Just Write!

Middle School Writing Prompts

Rachel Tolman Terry

© BlueHill Peak, 2019
ISBN: 9781798130704

Table of Contents

2 ... Animal Cage in Locker
4 ... Wright Brothers
6 ... Sloth Probs
8 ... Friend Moving
10 ... Magic Glasses
12 ... School Days Around the World
14 ... Hank's Piano Lesson
16 ... Bob's Diner
18 ... Slaty-Backed Forktails
20 ... John Lory and the Lighthouse
22 ... $50,000
24 ... Naming Streets
26 ... Necessary Machine
28 ... Lily's Camera Crew
30 ... School Club
32 ... Alien Tour
34 ... I'm a Snow Person
36 ... Hurricane Suitcase
38 ... Description of a Fictional Character
40 ... Patriotism
42 ... Help Neil
44 ... Squirrels in the Treehouse
46 ... Cave
48 ... New Best Friend
50 ... New Curriculum

52 ... Which 5 Things?
54 ... Mr. Oki's Cane
56 ... Which Job to Take?
58 ... Rock Star to Science Teacher?
60 ... Emergency Room Stories
62 ... International Trip
64 ... Choose a Sculpture
66 ... Zombie Apocalypse
68 ... Independence
70 ... Haunted House
72 ... Ruby's Illness
74 ... Harp at the Party
76 ... Mr. Pilsel's Paint Job
78 ... Anthony's Violin Case
80 ... Chess in the Park
82 ... Trapped!
84 ... Mummy!
86 ... Same Meal
88 ... Charles the Yorkie
90 ... Baby Decisions
92 ... Live Anywhere
94 ... Luck and Superstition
96 ... Mr. Rubio's Guinea Pig
98 ... Sandwich Time
100 ... Which Animal?

102 ... Bravery
104 ... What is True?
106 ... Cat
108 ... Cuthbert Brodrick
110 ... Treasure in the Trash
112 ... When You Were Younger
114 ... Season Poem
116 ... Objects
118 ... Follow the Penny
120 ... Friday Night
122 ... Bye Bye, Internet
124 ... Earliest Memory
126 ... Celebrity Yesterday
128 ... Object Transport
130 ... Email to the Future
132 ... Fortune Cookie
134 ... It's the Wolf's Turn
136 ... Kids Know
138 ... Feed Your Mind
140 ... Family Curse
142 ... Talents
144 ... New Shoes
146 ... Friend Attributes
148 ... Leo's Superpower
150 ... Living Forever
152 ... Working at the Zoo
154 ... Family Traditions
156 ... Game Time
158 ... Unique Architecture
160 ... Nick's Jump
162 ... Band Consultant
164 ... Abandoned Neighborhood
166 ... Amazing Burger
168 ... Miss O'Grady's Sketch Book
170 ... $1 Million for Others
172 ... Tanner's Friend
174 ... Creepy Old Puppet
176 ... Be Titus Salt
178 ... Tall Roommate
180 ... Rule to Live By
182 ... Dream Birthday
184 ... Start Feeling Happy Again
186 ... Young Mom or Dad
188 ... Secret Admirer
190 ... Sami's Ascent
192 ... Fears
194 ... Your Robot
196 ... Middle School Teacher
198 ... Most Comfy Chair
200 ... Stand Up

202 ... No Grocery Stores
204 ... Fashion Sense
206 ... Strange Compass
208 ... Work Instead of School
210 ... Relatives
212 ... New Holiday
214 ... Bed and Breakfast
216 ... Bonfire
218 ... Dream House
220 ... Hilda and the Spiders
222 ... Favorite Friend
224 ... Life without a SmartPhone
226 ... New Drone
228 ... Famous Artist
230 ... Leaf Fuel
232 ... Brief Convo
234 ... Boring Sam
236 ... Somewhere Else
238 ... Guiseppe and the Seizure
240 ... Refrigerator Probs
242 ... Letter for the Future
244 ... Living Underground
246 ... Valentine's Day Canceled
248 ... Story Time
250 ... First Day as an Apprentice

252 ... Alone Time
254 ... Halloween Costume
256 ... Separated at Birth
258 ... Astronaut Talk
260 ... Poor Quentin
262 ... Genevieve's Disappearance
264 ... Caterpillar Trouble
266 ... Your Choice
268 ... Up Close
270 ... In the Armoire
272 ... First Day Advice
274 ... Problem
276 ... Surfing
278 ... Cloud Shapes
280 ... Perfect Phone
282 ... Construction Site
284 ... Butterfly
286 ... Egg Hunt
288 ... Backyard Chickens
290 ... Hiding Place
292 ... Favorite Dessert
294 ... First Day of Spring
296 ... Satisfaction
298 ... Strange Creatures
300 ... Review

Learn more about our fab photographers on page 302 :)

ANIMAL CAGE IN LOCKER

After 3rd period, Nicholas stopped at his locker to pick up his math book, but when he opened his locker, he found a small animal cage where his math book should have been. He looked around to see if anyone was watching him. They weren't, so he opened the little door on the cage. Continue the story.

He closed his eyes. He was too scared to look. He felt a pinch and heard a chirp. He opened his eyes in the slightest bit. He saw a small bird. "What is your name" Nicholas asked the bird didn't respond obvoisly, he was a bird. He shut his locker and went on with his day.

WRIGHT BROTHERS

Orville and Wilbur Wright loved working on building projects when they were kids. Sometimes, when they were in the middle of a big project, their dad would let them stay home from school because he thought they would learn more from their projects than they would at school. What do you think about their dad's decision? Would you let your own children stay home from school to work on a project of their own?

SLOTH PROBS

Mango is a sloth who lives in a rainforest in Panama. Mango wants nothing more than to sleep for 20 hours a day and to eat for the other 4 hours, but an annoying gray-headed chachalaca keeps waking her up every ten minutes. This is interrupting Mango's dreams and driving her crazy. Something has to be done—and fast. What does Mango do?

Photograph: Ben Konfrst

Friend Moving

Your best friend moves away to a different state. You miss your friend, but you have other friends you can hang out with. Your friend, however, is really struggling to make new friends. Write a letter to your friend to offer encouragement and make suggestions about how to adjust to his or her new home.

Hey!
 I miss you so much. I love you! I am so so sorry you are having such a hard time meeting friends. But I have no doubt in this whole world that you wont. you will meet someone just as awesome and kind and beutiful as you! here is someways you could make freinds. JUST BE YOU!!! no one likes a fake!

MAGIC GLASSES

Something fishy is going on. Usually, Kate doesn't even bother raising her hand in class because she hardly ever knows the answers to the teachers' questions. Today, though, she's getting the answers right every time. The bell rings, and you accidentally spill the contents of your backpack on the floor. Everyone has left the classroom by the time you get your things together. On your way out, you notice a pair of glasses on a desk, Kate's desk. Wait, Kate doesn't wear glasses! You put the glasses on, and just then Mrs. Perez asks you, "What's on the lunch menu today?" A glowing green phrase appears on the lenses in front of your eyes. It says, "Spaghetti and meatballs, green beans, French bread." Just then, Kate comes running back into the classroom. She gasps, "The glasses!"

SCHOOL DAYS AROUND THE WORLD

Students in the United States attend school 180 days per year. In Bolivia, kids go to school 160 days each year, and in China students spend 260 days in school. Now you're in charge. What does the ideal school year look like? And how will you defend your decision to the students and their parents?

Photograph: Samuel Zeller

Hank's Piano Lesson

Normally, piano lessons were super boring. But on Thursday, while Hank was playing "Ode to Joy" for Mrs. Blue, the doorbell rang. "Excuse me, Hank," Mrs. Blue said. She opened the door, and two men in dark suits and sunglasses stood on the porch. One of them whispered in Mrs. Blue's ear and handed her a brown paper bag. Then, both men nodded their heads, spun around, and walked briskly back down the walkway. Hank peered through the sheer curtains and could see a shiny black Hummer speeding away down the street.

BOB'S DINER

Customers haven't been coming to Bob's Diner lately. First, a new restaurant opened up across the street that served out-of-this-world chicken fingers. Then, a shiny new pizzeria was built on the corner, and Bob saw more and more of his regular customers disappearing into the pizzeria's doors. What he needs is a new menu item that will bring back all of his old customers and attract new customers as well. He's hiring you to give his diner new life. What are your recommendations? How does it all turn out?

Photograph: R. Mac Wheeler

SLATY-BACKED FORKTAILS

Dr. Simpson travels to Nepal to study slaty-backed forktails. These birds live along the edges of fast-flowing rivers, and they eat little invertebrates they find among the rocks. One day, as Dr. Simpson is trying to record the calls of the slaty-backed forktails, one of the birds swoops down and grabs her recording device in its beak...

Photograph: Kannan AS

John Lory and the Lighthouse

When John Lory moved into the Pass A L'Outre lighthouse in the Mississippi Delta, the lighthouse was the tallest cast iron lighthouse in the United States. It was 1852, and John Lory was responsible for keeping the oil lamp burning all night long every night. Create another character and a challenge for John Lory and your new character to overcome.

Photograph: Cam Bradford

$50,000

You have just won $50,000! What will you do with the money? How will your life be different because of your prize?

Photograph: Vladimir Solomyani

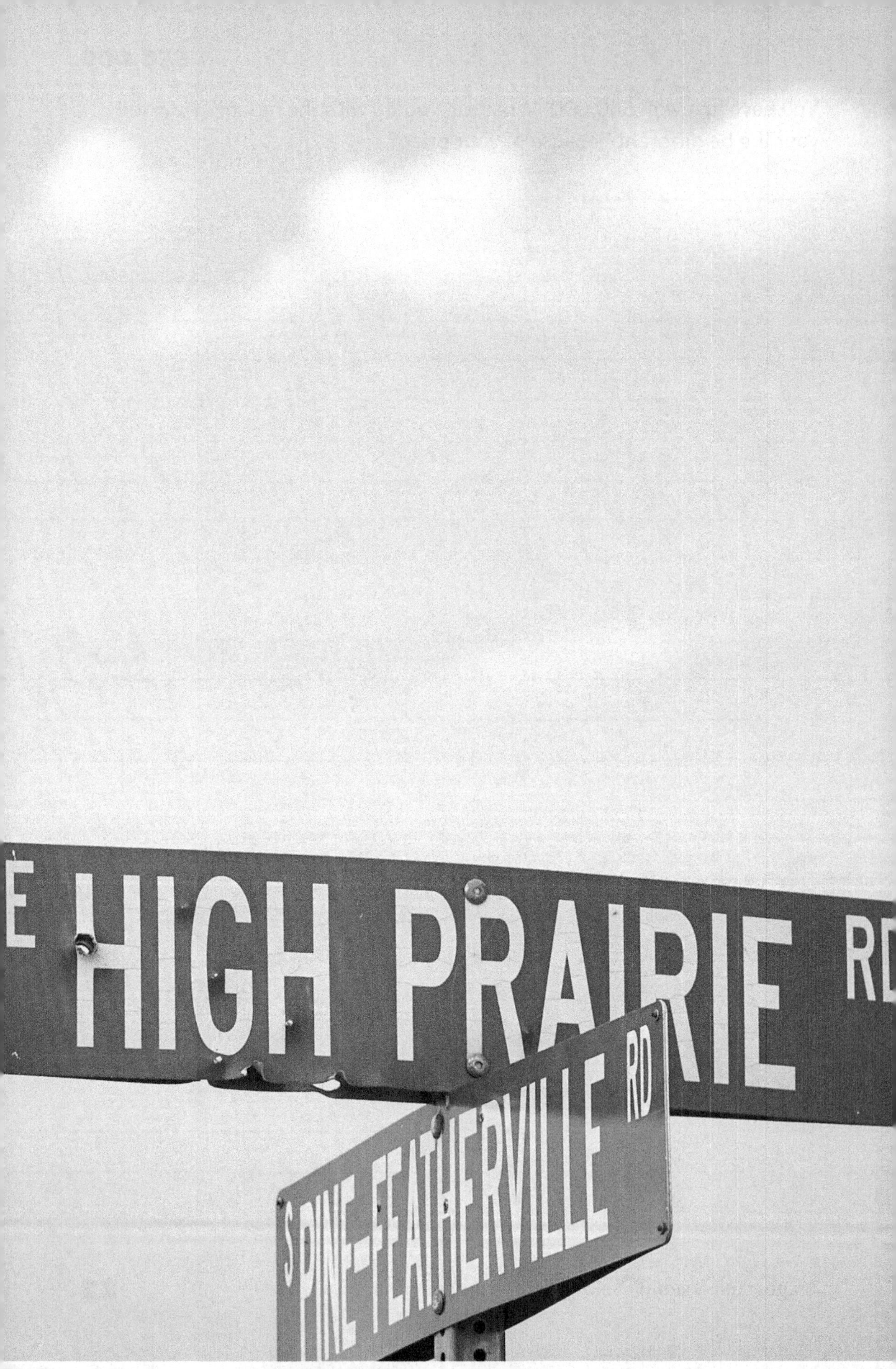
E HIGH PRAIRIE RD
S PINE-FEATHERVILLE RD

Naming Streets

The mayor of your city has asked you to rename three streets. Which three streets will you rename? Choose names for the three streets, and explain why you choose those names.

Necessary Machine

You use a lot of machines every day. Make a list of all the machines you use, and then choose the machine that you wouldn't want to live without. How would your life be different if you didn't have that machine.

Lily's Camera Crew

Lily didn't fit in with the rest of the kids in her class. She wore strange clothes, and she had a habit of repeating the last three words of other people's sentences. Nobody wanted to hang out with her at lunch until that strange Wednesday in October when a camera crew followed Lily into the lunchroom.

School Club

You're in charge of starting a new club for your school. What will your club be called? What will club members do? How will you get kids to come to your club?

Photograph: Alexis Brown

30

Alien Tour

A UFO has landed in your backyard, and an alien has emerged from the spacecraft. He seems friendly enough, and he'd like you to escort him around your community. Plan out a tour of your town, and explain the five most important stops on your tour.

I'm a Snow Person

You're a snowman (or snow woman). Explain what it feels like to be formed, decorated, and left out in the cold. Don't forget to talk about what it's like to start melting when the weather warms up.

Photograph: Eberhard Grossgasteiger

Hurricane Suitcase

A hurricane is heading right toward your house! Your mom tells you that you need to pack one suitcase full of your most important possessions to take with you when you evacuate. What will you put in your suitcase?

DESCRIPTION OF A FICTIONAL CHARACTER

Write a physical description of your favorite fictional character. It can be a character from a book, a movie, a TV show, or even a song.

PATRIOTISM

What makes you proud to be a citizen of your country?

Photograph: Vladislav Klapin

Help Neil

When you see Neil after school, he looks like he has something very serious on his mind. What has happened? How can you help?

SQUIRRELS IN THE TREEHOUSE

Lindsay and Mason discover an abandoned treehouse in the woods, and they start meeting there every Saturday after their chores are done. One day, when they arrive at the treehouse, they find a circle of squirrels chattering away inside the treehouse. One of the squirrels notices the boys and points at them. Lindsay and Mason try to creep back down the tree unnoticed, but it's too late.

CAVE

The day started out beautiful, so Nick and Theo decided to go for a hike in the mountains. About an hour into their hike, though, clouds rolled in and the sky grew dark. Before long, it was raining, and they hadn't brought any rain gear. Huddling beneath the branches of a large pine tree, Theo noticed an unusually large hole in the ground. The boys discovered that it was a cave, and with the lightning and thunder coming ever closer, they wiggled into the cave and found themselves in a magnificent cavern!

Photograph: Jared Rice

NEW BEST FRIEND

A new family moves in next door, and one of the kids is just your age! This kid is the friend of your dreams. How does this person look? Behave? Favorite subjects in school? Hobbies? What will you do together? How will you meet?

New Curriculum

Sam has just moved to a new area, and he shows up for the first day of school. His teacher announces that students will no longer have to learn mathematics or writing. Instead, they'll learn how to make bricks so the town can build watch towers. How does Sam feel about this? Why would his new school do such a thing?

Which 5 Things?

A tornado is headed for your house, and you only have time to stuff five things in a bag to take with you to the shelter. Which five things do you take?

Mr. Oki's Cane?

Mr. Oki uses a wooden cane when he walks, and it's the most unusual cane you ever saw. Describe the cane and explain how Mr. Oki got it.

Which Job to Take??

You've been offered two jobs. The first job is feeding towels into a towel-folding machine for three hours each day after school. The second job is scrubbing graffiti off the walls in your city for 6 hours on Friday and 6 hours on Saturday. You have to take one of the jobs because you need to buy your school books. Which job do you take? Why? Describe your first day on the job.

Rock Star to Science Teacher?

Sarah finds out that her boring old science teacher used to be a guitarist in a band! Explain the teacher's path from rock star to science teacher.

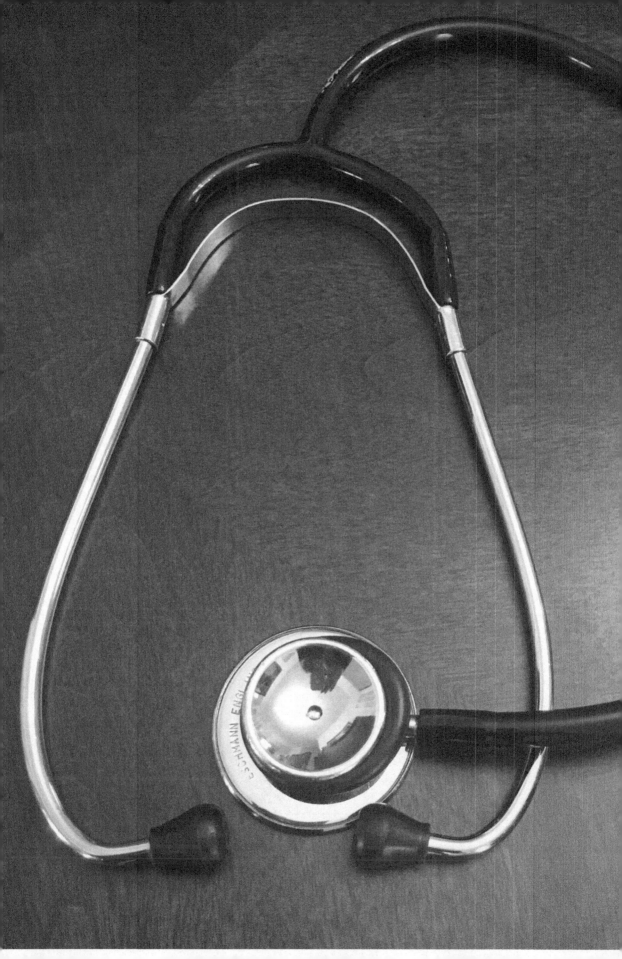

EMERGENCY ROOM STORIES

Dr. Wexman works in an Emergency Room and hears all kinds of crazy stories about how people got injured. Lucy goes to the Emergency Room because she has a baby tooth stuck in her ear. Write the story that she will tell Dr. Wexman about how the tooth got there.

INTERNATIONAL TRIP

If you could visit another country, which country would you visit? What would you like to do on your trip? How long would you like to stay? Whom would you take with you?

Photograph: Amarnath Tade

CHOOSE A SCULPTURE

You've been chosen to create a sculpture for your city's town hall. Describe what your sculpture will look like, what materials you'll use, and why you think this is a great sculpture for your city. After you're done describing your sculpture, draw a picture of it.

City's New Statue

ZOMBIE APOCALYPSE

The Zombie Apocalypse has begun. Which of your friends or classmates will be the best leader to get everyone safely through it? What one weapon will you use during the Apocalypse? Where will you have your hideout? How will you communicate with your allies?

INDEPENDENCE

What if you didn't have any parents or guardians? Where would you live? How would you earn money? What would your daily schedule look like?

Haunted House

You're in charge of planning the haunted house for the neighborhood Halloween party. Write about five rooms in the haunted house and how you plan on scaring everyone silly. You can also draw a floorplan of what your haunted house will look like.

Haunted House Floorplan

Ruby's Illness

Ruby sat nervously in the waiting room at her doctor's office. Her head hurt and she felt weak and sweaty. Worst of all, purple bumps had sprung up all over her arms and legs. When the nurse came to fetch her, she looked at Ruby's arms and said, "Oh no, not another one. You're the seventh one today."

How did Ruby catch this disease? What is it called, and how will Ruby's doctor treat it? Will Ruby be okay? Will she have any long-lasting problems because of it?

Photograph: Aiony Haust

HARP AT THE PARTY

Catrin played the harp, and even though she was only 14, people hired her to play calm and relaxing music at their weddings. One day, however, Catrin got an interesting request. A woman called and asked her if she could play at her 4-year-old son's birthday party.

"I'm sorry," Catrin said, "Did you say you want me to play for 4-year-old boys?"

"Yes, that's right," the woman said. "I'm hoping it will help them to be calm."

"Hmm," Catrin said.

"I'll pay you double what you normally charge," the woman said.

"Deal," Catrin said.

Write about the birthday party.

Photograph: Heidi Yanulis

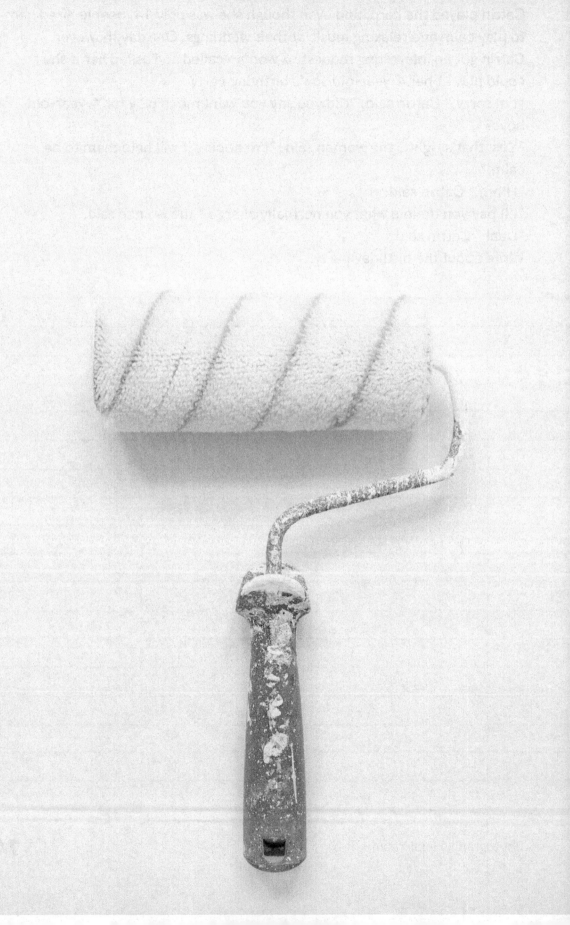

Mr. Pilsel's Paint Job

Arthur sometimes helped his father with his painting business, and he was pretty happy with his newfound skills. He arrived with his dad at a new job site, an old Victorian house, and they met with the owner, Mister Pilsel.

"I want every room to be a different color," Mister Pilsel said.

"We can do whatever you want," Arthur's dad assured the old man.

"Orange. Blue. Green. Red. And so on," Mister Pilsel said.

Arthur's dad made notes in his notebook. "Right," he said.

"And the paint in each room should smell like its color," the man said.

"Smell?" Arthur's dad asked.

"Yes," Mister Pilsel said.

Finish the story.

Photograph: Yoann Siloine

ANTHONY'S VIOLIN CASE

Anthony carried a violin case to school every day. But he didn't go to orchestra, and no one had ever seen him playing a violin.
What does Anthony keep inside his violin case? And what's the big secret anyway?

Chess in the Park

Micah and Jo were playing chess in the park when a bird flew by and snatched Jo's queen in its beak. They were both too stunned to do anything about it.

Less than a minute later, a different bird flew by and dropped the queen right on the chess board, scattering the other pieces.

Finish the story.

TRAPPED!

You're trapped in an elevator! Who's with you? What resources do you have? And what's your plan for getting out? Write all about it.

Mummy!

If a mummy could talk, what would it tell you?

Photograph: Isabella Juskova

SAME MEAL

If you had to eat the same meal every day for the rest of your life, what would it be? Explain why each part of the meal is important. Would you ever get tired of it? If so, how soon?

Charles the Yorkie

Mrs. Jones has a purebred Yorkshire terrier named Charles. Unlike the other dogs on the street, Charles eats real people food, sleeps on a silk pillow, and visits the groomer once a week for a bath and thorough brushing. The trouble is, Charles wants to be like the other dogs, and he doesn't care one bit about his pedigree (which hangs on the wall of Mrs. Jones's living room).

What will Charles do to live the life he's always wanted?

Baby Decisions

What if babies had to be consulted about the decisions parents make for them? For instance, what if babies got to choose their own names? Decide what to wear? Pick out their own baby food? Choose their own schedules? Write a story to illustrate what life would be like if babies got to make all their own decisions.

LIVE ANYWHERE

If you could choose to live anywhere in the world (and you would automatically be able to speak the language there), where would you choose? Explain your decision.

Luck and Superstition

Some people think that carrying around a rabbit's foot will bring good luck. Some believe that it's a bad omen when a black cat crosses their paths. Some refuse to walk underneath ladders because they think something bad will happen. All of these are superstitions. Do you have any superstitions? If you don't, why not?

MR. RUBIO'S GUINEA PIG

Mr. Rubio brought a guinea pig to school and said it was going to be the class pet. Everyone seemed to like the pig, and some students started to bring it lettuce and herbs for treats. One morning, the students arrived to find two guinea pigs in the cage.

"All right," Mr. Rubio said, "who's the jokester?"

The students looked around the classroom, but no one seemed to know what their teacher was talking about.

"Who brought the other guinea pig in?" Mr. Rubio asked.

Everyone was silent.

Write a story to explain how the second guinea pig got in the cage.

Sandwich Time

List Time: Make a list of 30 different sandwich flavors. These have to be sandwiches you would actually eat yourself, even if you've never yet tried them all.

WHICH ANIMAL?

If you had to live as a sheep, a chicken, or a pig, which would you choose? Why?

Bravery

What's the bravest thing you've ever done? Do you think you could be brave enough to do it again if you had to?

WHAT IS TRUE?

What is something you know to be true? How do you know it's true? How would you respond if someone told you that it wasn't true?

Cat

Name this cat. Give him (or her) a story, a home (or not), a past, a goal. Tell a good story about this cat!

Photograph: Callum Wale

CUTHBERT BRODRICK

His name is Cuthbert Brodrick. Write a complete description of this character, including what he looks like, what he sounds like, what he wears, where he lives, and what makes him unique.

Photograph: Na Inho

TREASURES IN THE TRASH

If there was one thing Matt loved, it was finding treasures in the trash. His bedroom was full of interesting items he had pulled out of garbage bins, found on the street, and collected from the junk yard. Write about Matt's five favorite items and how he found them.

When You Were Younger

What is something you loved to do when you were younger that you haven't done for a long time? When did you stop doing it? Do you think it would be fun to try it again?

SEASON POEM

Write a poem about your favorite season. It doesn't have to rhyme, but it can if you want it to. Make sure you use details that help the reader to feel, see, smell, taste, and hear the season.

OBJECTS

Take a look around you right now. Choose an object that you can see, and write about its history. How old is it? Who has used it before? What purpose does it serve? Why is it in its current location? Is it valuable or special to anyone?

FOLLOW THE PENNY

Follow a penny as it makes its way through five different owners. How is it used? What does it help buy? How long does it stay with each person?

Friday Night

What is your favorite way to spend Friday night?

BYE BYE, INTERNET

The Internet is going to crash tomorrow, and it's never going to come back. How will your life be different? What will you miss? In what ways will your life be better? Worse?

Earliest Memory

Write about your earliest memory. How old do you think you were? Who else was there? Do you think your memory is accurate?

CELEBRITY YESTERDAY

Think of your favorite celebrity. Now think about what happened yesterday. Insert your favorite celebrity into what happened yesterday. Be creative with your story, but keep some of the realistic elements from what really happened.

OBJECT TRANSPORT

Look around the room and choose an object that you've never really noticed before. Now transport that object to the year 1800. What would people in 1800 think of that object? Would they know what to do with it? Write a story about a person in 1800 discovering that object and figuring out how to use it.

Email to the Future

Write an email to yourself to read ten years from now. Where are you hoping you'll be? What do you hope you'll be doing? Be encouraging to yourself.

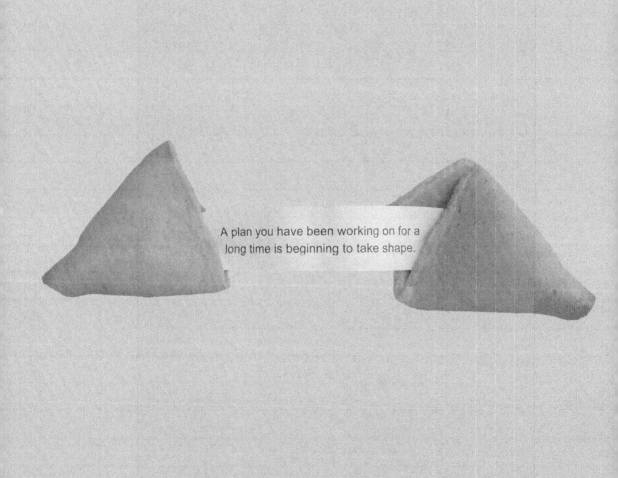

FORTUNE COOKIE

You open this fortune cookie on Wednesday. What happens on Thursday? Explain the plan and how it took shape, but make sure there's a big hiccup in the plan.

It's the Wolf's Turn

Rewrite "Little Red Riding Hood" from the wolf's perspective.

KIDS KNOW

What things do all kids know that adults do not?

Feed Your Mind

You feed your body in order to have energy and strength. You also feed your mind. What kinds of things do you feed your mind every day? Make a list of the things you feed your mind and then write about things you would like to add to your "mind diet."

Photograph: Samuel Zeller

Family Curse

One night, Kate's great-great grandmother appears to her in a dream and tells her about a curse that a mean old neighbor placed on the family many years ago. Kate's great-great grandmother tells Kate that she's the only person who can break the curse. What is the curse? And how will Kate break it?

TALENTS

What is your greatest talent? What is your greatest weakness? How can you turn your weakness into a strength?

New Shoes

If you could have any pair of shoes you want, what would it be? How would your new shoes improve your life?

Photograph: James Baldwin

FRIEND ATTRIBUTES

What is more important in a friend: a good sense of humor or the ability to keep secrets? Why?

Leo's Superpower

Leo was on his way to baseball practice when the biggest bully in town grabbed his baseball mitt and threw it high into a tree. That's when Leo discovered that he suddenly had a superpower. What superpower does Leo have? How does he use it? And does the bully bother him anymore?

LIVING FOREVER

If you could live forever but the people around you had normal lifespans, how would you adapt? What would you do when your friends grew old but you stayed young? How would you use your time? What would be your mission in life?

Photograph: Jana Sabeth Schultz

Working at the Zoo

If you worked at a zoo, what kind of job would you like to do? Create a shift schedule showing what kinds of tasks you'll do in your job.

FAMILY TRADITIONS

What are your favorite family traditions? Which traditions could you do without? Which family traditions will you continue with your own children in the future?

GAME TIME

What is your favorite game to play? How often do you play it? With whom do you like to play? Why do you think you like it so much?

Unique Architecture

You're an architect, and you've been commissioned to design a building that will be constructed out of a unique material. The person commissioning the project wants the building to be one of a kind, a monument to innovation and ingenuity. Draw a picture of your building design, and then write about what makes it so unique. What materials will you use? How will it be constructed?

Photograph: Konrad Wojciechowski

NICK'S JUMP

This is Nick. Just before he launched himself down the slope for his final jump in the national ski jumping championship, he remembered that he had promised to take Sara out for dinner at 7:00 this evening. It's 6:45. He's been trying to get Sara to go out with him for a year, and she finally said yes for the first time. What's going to happen next?

Photograph: Todd Trapani

Band Consultant

Your favorite band needs a consultant to help them design their next tour. Give them advice on their stage set, their new songs, the cities they should go to on tour, and what they should wear during their concerts.

Abandoned Neighborhood

Imagine what your neighborhood would look like if everyone left it tomorrow and never came back. What would it look like in one year? Ten years? Fifty years? A thousand years? What kind of situation could cause everyone to leave it and not return?

Photograph: Florian Olivo

Amazing Burger

You show up at the school cafeteria, expecting the same tasteless slice of pizza when the lunch lady hands you this.
You look confused, but she simply smiles and says, "Next!"
What has happened back there in the kitchen? Explain how this amazing hamburger showed up in the cafeteria.

Photograph: Edward Guk

Miss O'Grady's Sketch Book

Every afternoon at three o'clock, Miss O'Grady takes her sketch book and her favorite pencil box across the street to the park. She sits on the same bench every day and watches the children come home from school. As they walk past her, she sketches them.

One sunny Thursday, one of the boys distracts her by acting like a monkey. As she's watching him, another boy grabs Miss O'Grady's sketch book and runs away. What do they discover as they flip through the pages? Where does their discovery lead?

$1 Million for Others

If you had $1,000,000, but you couldn't spend it on yourself, what would you do with it?

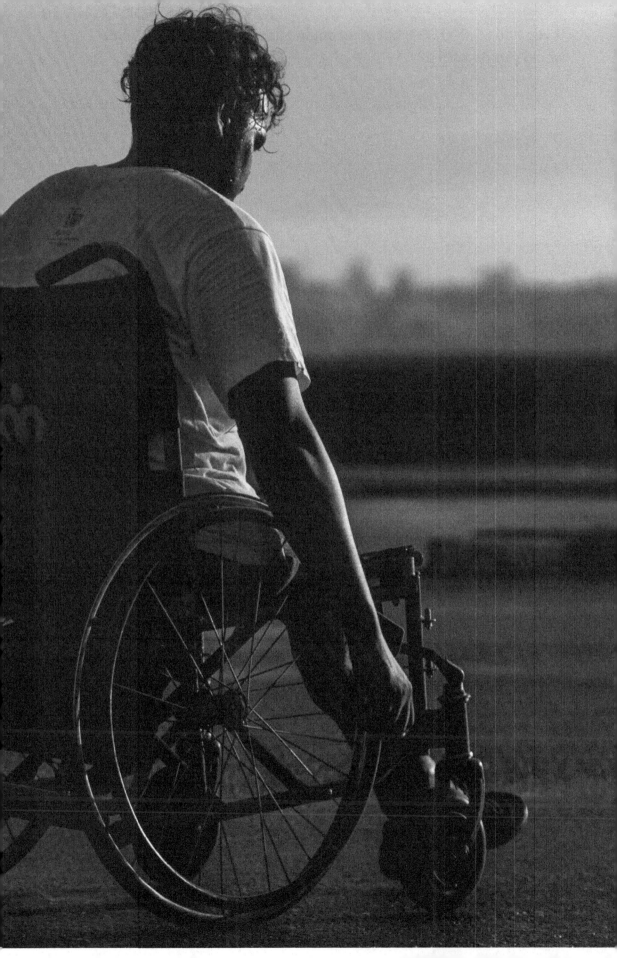

TANNER'S FRIEND

On his way home from Cal's house, Tanner was hit by a car. When he woke up, he realized that his legs were paralyzed. Put yourself in Cal's place and think about what you can do to help your friend. What will you say to him the first time you visit him in the hospital? What will you do to help Tanner as he tries to get his life back to normal?

CREEPY OLD PUPPET

While you're helping your grandma to clean out her attic, you discover a creepy old puppet. You think it might be fun to use to scare your little sister, so you take it home and put it in your closet. That night, you wake up to discover the puppet talking to you.
What happens next?

BE TITUS SALT

Titus Salt founded a city in Yorkshire, England, in the 1850s. The city was called "Saltaire," named after Titus Salt and the Aire River, which runs through the town. He built a mill for producing wool cloth, and thousands of people worked there. He also built a school, a hospital, a town hall, hundreds of houses for the workers, a dining hall, and a church.

If you could start a town of your own, what would you call it? What kind of work would be available for the town residents to do? What kinds of buildings would you include in your town? What would it look like?

TALL ROOMMATE

It's your first day of college, and you're excited about meeting your roommate and going to your classes. You come back from classes to discover that your roommate has already moved in. Everything that belongs to your roommate is huge! You're trying to figure out what's going on when your new roommate comes in and you understand why: he or she is 9 feet tall!

Write about the advantages and disadvantages of having a roommate who is 9 feet tall.

Rule to Live By

What is the most important rule to live by?

Photograph: Javier Allegue Barros

DREAM BIRTHDAY

Describe your dream birthday party. Where would it be? Who would be there? Describe every last detail.

START FEELING HAPPY AGAIN

What's the best way to start feeling happy again after you've had a disappointment?

YOUNG MOM OR DAD

Travel back in time and hang out with your mom or dad when she or he was the age you are now. What will you spend the day doing? What questions will you ask? What will you say?

Secret Admirer

There's a letter for you in the mail. Here's what it says,

To My Dearest Beloved,

I see you every day, but I'm too shy to tell you how I feel. When the sky is gray, all I have to do is think of you and then it's like the sun has returned to my world. I feel it's time to reveal my identity. Will you meet me on the corner of Maple and Main this Tuesday at 3:30pm?

Yours Truly,

???

What's your next step? Do you go to the corner of Maple and Main on Tuesday? What happens next?

Photograph: Bundo Kim

Sami's Ascent

This is Sami Antar. Two years ago, he was staying with his friend Gil because he didn't have an apartment of his own. Today, he owns an entire apartment building. How did he come so far in the past two years? Write Sami's story.

Photograph: Ali Morshedlou

FEARS

What were you afraid of when you were little? What are you afraid of now?

Your Robot

The robot is nearly done. Your client is going to be using it to perform dangerous tasks in a decommissioned nuclear power plant. But if you could keep the robot, you would use it to do other things. Write about how you would use the robot and what you would teach it to do.

Middle School Teacher

If you were a middle school teacher, which subject would you teach? What kind of teacher would you be? Describe a day in your classroom.

Most Comfy Chair

You're an innovative furniture designer, and you've been asked to design the world's most comfortable chair. What materials will you use? How will you construct it? What will make your chair design unique and different from all the chair previously designed?

STAND UP

Write about three things that are worth standing up for. Why are they so important to you? What would happen if you didn't stand up for them?

No Grocery Stores

What would you do if you couldn't buy food from grocery stores? How would you get your food? What would you eat? What foods would you miss the most that you take for granted now?

Fashion Sense

You have an unlimited budget for buying an outfit to wear to your friend's party on Friday. What will you wear? Be as specific as possible.

STRANGE COMPASS

Michael sees something shiny on the sidewalk up ahead. He gets closer to it and sees that it's a compass, but it's not like any compass he has seen before. Since he's in a hurry, he puts it in his pocket so he can examine it by and by.

Later in the day, he's walking home when an elderly woman approaches him and asks him how to get to the post office. He points up the road and says, "Just walk up that way, and when you get to Park Lane, turn north." As soon as he says the word "north," Michael's stomach drops as if he were on a roller coaster and he finds himself in a stormy, blue-and-white landscape...

WORK INSTEAD OF SCHOOL

Imagine that you're living 150 years ago and that you come from a poor family. You'll have to stop going to school and start working to contribute to your family's finances. What kind of work will you do? Do you think you'll miss school? Do you think you'll continue to learn from your work?

Relatives

Think of a person in your extended family (a cousin, aunt, uncle, grandmother, grandfather, etc.). What do you have in common with this person? What differences do you have? Would someone be able to tell that you're relatives?

New Holiday

Invent a new nationally recognized holiday. On what day will the new holiday be celebrated? What kinds of festivities will people participate in? Will there be any special foods? Symbols? Gatherings? Community events?

Bed and Breakfast

Tim and his family stayed at a bed and breakfast on their vacation, and he had never been to a bed and breakfast before. His room was comfortable but a little strange. It was filled with books and plants, and there was a cat that showed up periodically. He felt like he was staying in someone else's bedroom. In the morning at breakfast, the host told Tim

BONFIRE

Nick and Lucy decided that the best way to celebrate Halloween would be to light a giant bonfire in the empty lot behind the burger place. They started collecting shipping pallets and stacking them up in the middle of the empty lot. The night before Halloween, they met at the empty lot to arrange the pallets in a pyramid for their bonfire. As they stacked them up, they noticed that someone had written letters on the pallets, and the letters started to form words as they stacked them.

Finish the story.

DREAM HOUSE

Where would you build your dream house? What would it look like? How many rooms would it have? After you finish writing about your dream house, draw either a floor plan or a drawing of the home's exterior.

Hilda and the Spiders

Hilda finds that most people just don't have an open mind when it comes to spiders. They either try to smash them with their shoes or they run away from them. Hilda, on the other hand, thinks spiders are beautiful. With their delicate legs and interesting eyes, they're some of Nature's most interesting creatures. So why is everyone so afraid of them?

That's what Hilda is thinking as she pulls her jar of spiders out of her backpack on Monday morning. Continue the story.

Photograph: Matthew Cabret

Favorite Friend

Write about your favorite friend. What makes this friend so special to you? How long have you known this person? Include some stories about your friend in your response.

Photograph: Antonino Visalli

LIFE WITHOUT A SMARTPHONE

If you didn't have a television, a computer, a smartphone, or any other digital devices, how would you communicate with your friends? What would you do with your free time?

Photograph: Luke Porter

New Drone

Paulo got a drone for Christmas, and he couldn't wait to get it up in the air. But the weather was crummy on Christmas Day and even worse the day after that. By the time he could finally take his drone outside, he was determined to fly it somewhere amazing…

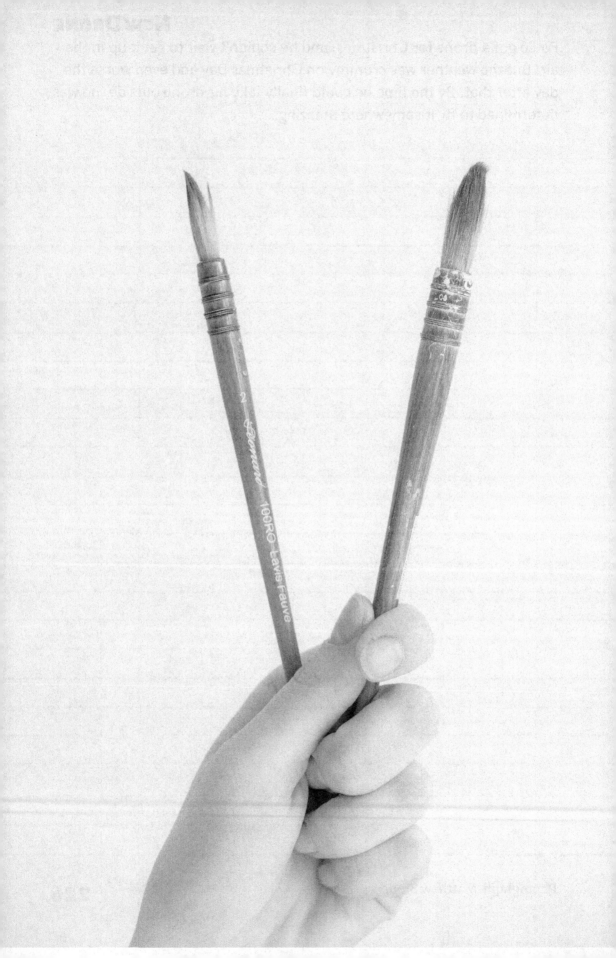

Famous Artist

If you were a famous artist, what kind of artwork would you create? Describe your art, and then tell where you would like to exhibit it.

LEAF FUEL

Mr. and Mrs. Henery have figured out a way to turn dead tree leaves into fuel for their car, but they only have two small trees on their property. How will Mr. and Mrs. Henery get enough leaves to keep their car running year round?

Photograph: Annie Spratt

Brief Convo

You're on your way to the bus stop when you hear an unusual conversation somewhere overhead. Looking up, you see these two birds.

Record their conversation and then tell what happens next.

BORING SAM

Sam has always lived in the same town on the same street in the same house. His family always eats tacos on Tuesday, chicken soup on Wednesday, and fish sticks on Thursday. Sam always wears a grey shirt, blue jeans, and white shoes to school. And he eats a peanut butter sandwich every day of the week.

But one day, a Tuesday, Sam shows up at school wearing an orange shirt, and at lunch, he pulls an egg salad sandwich out of his lunch bag.

What's going on?

Photograph: Flavius Les

SOMEWHERE ELSE

Tell ya what. I won't tell your teacher that you're wishing you were somewhere else. But you have to promise to write where else you'd rather be. Here. I got some paper for you.

Guiseppe and the Seizure

Giuseppe has gotten really good at baseball over the summer. He's been playing catch with his dad and his older brother, and he goes to the batting cages on Saturday afternoons. He tries out for one of the city teams and makes it.

In fact, things are going so well that the coach makes Guiseppe the starting pitcher.

In his very first game as starting pitcher, Guiseppe strikes out the first five batters, but then something happens. Suddenly, right before throwing a pitch, Guiseppe falls down and starts shaking. He doesn't know what's happening, and his teammates don't know either. Later on, Guiseppe learns that he's had a seizure and that he has a condition that can cause seizures to happen at any time. Some of the kids on his team make fun of him, and he is very embarrassed.

What should Guiseppe do? Should he continue to play baseball? Will his life be changed forever?

Photograph: Keith Johnston

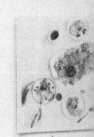

REFRIGERATOR PROBS

Your refrigerator stops working, and you're no longer able to keep food cold in your house. How will this affect your life? What will you miss? How will you deal with not having a refrigerator?

LETTER FOR THE FUTURE

Write a letter to your great-great-great grandchildren to tell them what life is like for you now. What do you think they will find interesting? In what ways do you think their lives will be like yours? How do you think their lives will be different? What advice will you give them?

Photograph: Brad Neathery

Living Underground

Aliens from outer space have taken over the surface of the earth, and all the remaining humans have moved underground. What is your new underground community like? How do you eat? Is it necessary to create light? If so, how do you do it? What other problems do the underground humans need to overcome?

VALENTINE'S DAY CANCELED

Valentine's Day has been canceled because there's a sugar shortage and love has died. Is there any way to revive love and bring back Valentine's Day? Create a campaign to bring the love back.

Story Time

Write a story using this photograph as inspiration. Don't forget to include a beginning, middle, and end to your story, and make sure there's a conflict to be resolved.

First Day as an Apprentice

It's 1840, and Abraham has just been apprenticed to his Uncle John who is a tailor. It's his first official day of work, and Abraham is nervous, even though he has always loved his uncle. On his way to Uncle John's workshop, he trips and falls in the mud, but there's no time to go home and get cleaned up. Write about Abraham's first day as an apprentice.

Alone Time

Where is your favorite place to be alone? Why do you like to be there? What do you do? Use plenty of descriptive words to tell your readers exactly what it's like.

Halloween Costume

What was your favorite Halloween costume? How did you come up with the costume? What did you feel like when you were wearing it? Why do you think you liked it so much?

SEPARATED AT BIRTH

Caroline doesn't know that she has a twin because they were separated at birth. How does Caroline find out that she has a twin? What is her twin like? Are they identical or fraternal? How will their lives change now that they know about each other?

Photograph: Felipe Bustillo

Astronaut Talk

Write a text message conversation between an astronaut and an extra-terrestrial from another planet.

Poor Quentin

Quentin is sick to death of being dressed up in these ridiculous outfits. It's time to assert some independence. It's time to make his voice heard! What does Quentin do?

Photograph: Charles Deluvio

Genevieve's Disappearance

This is Eberhard's Hotel. Genevieve stayed here last night. Her window was the top one on the left. It appears that Genevieve disappeared sometime in the night. All that remains in her room this morning is an empty shopping bag, a pair of tweezers, and a book entitled, *1001 Useful Romanian Phrases*.

Since you're in charge of the investigation, you've got to get to work. Whom will you question? What clues will you seek? How will you proceed?

Also, write a paragraph from Genevieve's point of view (the investigator doesn't have to know about it).

Photograph: Felix Arauner

CATERPILLAR TROUBLE

Joseph Cameron serves as a sentry at the Tower of London. He must stand very still and very straight during his post. One day, a tiny green caterpillar approaches him during his shift. It seems to contemplate him for a while, and then it slowly but steadily creeps up his shiny boot and makes its way all the way up his slacks, his shirt, and up to his collar. What does he do?

Photograph: Bart Christiaanse

Your Choice

Create a story to go with this picture.

Photograph: Averie Woodard

UP CLOSE

Write about what you see in this picture. Describe it from any point of view you like.

Photograph: Wolfgang Hasselman

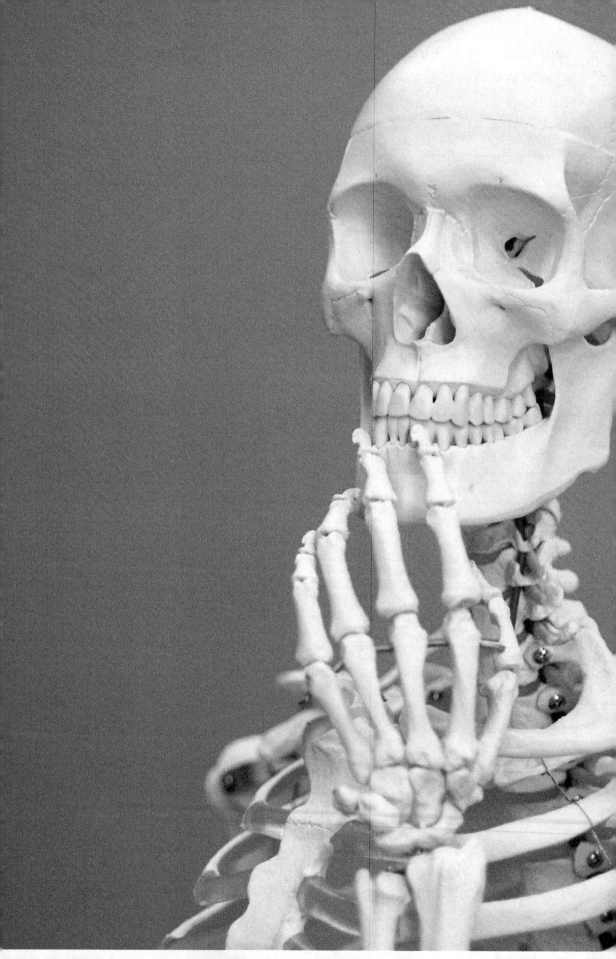

In the Armoire

Pete and Greta had been volunteered (by their dad) to help their neighbor, Mrs. Williams, clean out her attic. It was hot and dusty up there, and they were getting tired of carrying boxes of musty clothing down the attic stairs.

Late in the afternoon, Pete opened up the creaky old door of an armoire that leaned against one wall, and gasped. There was a skeleton inside!

First Day Advice

What advice will you give your grandchildren before they attend their first day of middle school? What do you wish you had known?

Problem

What do you think is the biggest problem facing people your age? Have you thought of any solutions to the problem?

SURFING

Write about everything that happened in the day leading up to this ride. Then tell what happened afterward.

Cloud Shapes

You're lying on your back on a quilt in the park, and you see these very clouds up above you. What shapes can you make out? What objects do they resemble? Once you figure it out, write a story about one of the shapes.

Photograph: Kenrick Mills

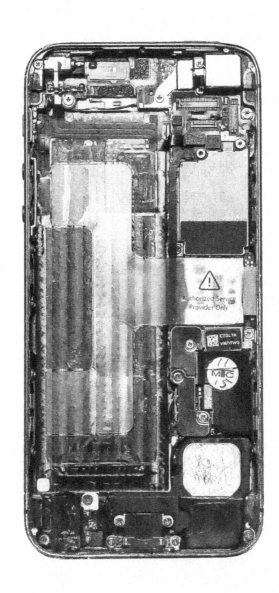

PERFECT PHONE

You've been tasked with designing the world's most perfect phone. What will it be like? What features will it have? Why are these features important? How will you convince people to buy it?

Construction Site

Leo has been working as an apprentice on a construction site. Everyone saw him earlier in the day, but now they can't find him anywhere. What happened?

Butterfly

Nothing was going right. I couldn't find my shoes this morning. There was no milk in the fridge for my cereal. My best friend didn't wait for me to walk to school. I left my homework on the kitchen table. The school bully knocked me over in the hallway. And then this happened (see the photo). What does it mean? And what changes because of it? Write about the rest of the day.

Egg Hunt

Ellie felt like she was too old to participate in the neighborhood Easter egg hunt, but her little brother had pleaded and pleaded with her until she agreed to go with him.

All the kids lined up at one end of the park and then Mr. Quillen said, "Go!" Bright plastic eggs started filling the kids' baskets, and soon they were slowing down, unable to find more eggs. That's when Ellie's little brother pointed out something shiny and golden in the rosebush by the statue...

Backyard Chickens

What do you think about people keeping chickens in their backyards in the city? Do you think it's a good idea? What are the pros and cons of backyard chickens? Who might be affected by chickens in the city? And how could they be affected?

Hiding Place

What is the best hiding place you've ever found? Have you used it? Does anyone else know about it? Write in detail about the hiding place.

Favorite Dessert

What is your favorite kind of dessert? Do you get to eat it often? Do you know how to make it? Try to describe your favorite dessert to someone who has never tasted it before.

First Day of Spring

It's been a long, hard winter, but today finally feels like the first day of Spring! Describe everything you see, hear, smell, feel, and taste as you go exploring on this magical morning.

Satisfaction

When do you feel the most satisfied with your life? If you haven't felt content with how your life is going, what can you do to make improvements?

Strange Creatures

What is the strangest creature you've ever seen? Where did you see it? How is it different from other animals you've seen?

REVIEW

Read back through your writing and choose your favorite piece. Analyze it and come up with five things you like about it and three ways you would improve it if you wrote it today. Then write yourself a hearty congratulations for finishing this book. You're a better writer now than when you started. I'm proud of you!

Photograph: Hannah Olinger

Photographer Bios

Spike Allibone
Spike is a 'left of field' human with esoteric people skills. Most people really like him. He takes photos of beautiful people and really must stop talking nonsense.

Jeremy Bishop
I first found my passion for photography by shooting surf with the GoPro. Being a waterman has opened my eye to the unique patterns and textures in nature, and my goal is to capture those fleeting moments.

Chase Clark
Chase is a designer living in Boston who loves playing with cameras, running and spending time with his family.

Jack Catalano
Jack Catalano attends high-school in Orange County, California. He enjoys vacations with family, playing video games with friends, and studying science and engineering. He also loves photography, which he has pursued since fifth grade.

Deleece Cook
Deleece Cook is an Artist, Photographer & Film Maker who specialises in the Mystical, and who resides in scenic Blue Mountains, New South Wales, Australia.

Josue Escoto
I'm a designer and photographer from Honduras. I grew up in a poor family, but nothing made me stop following my dream. Now I'm living it. Follow your dream!

Bennett Dungan
Bennett Dungan is a web developer from Louisiana who enjoys venturing out on the weekends to take photos of scenic landscape and space.

John Fowler
John Fowler retired from his job as a physicist to follow his lifelong dream of photography, which he learned as a boy from his mother.

Eberhard Grossgasteiger
I am a trained network technician, web developer and photographer. I work as an independent freelancer. My hobbies are sports in general, photography and creativity!

Terrah Holly
Northern native enjoying the warm south. Photography is my catalyst to discover, explore, document, and create beautiful things. I'm alive when I'm rising through the mountains or falling into the waves.

Carly Jayne
Carly Jayne started taking pictures of food for local restaurants 8 years ago. Little did she know it would develop into a business called Love Like Salt! She now resides in Portland, Oregon with her two kids, husband and sweet senior dog.

Isabella Juscová

Isabella Jusková is a graphic designer based in Toronto, Canada, with a passion for photography and the wild. She is a traveller, a promoter of sustainability and animal welfare.

Roman Kraft

Kraft is the photographer & maker behind band&roll • a family workshop making quality goods for pets and their humans.

Elena Koycheva

Elena Koycheva is a content creator and photographer, born and raised in Bulgaria, and currently based in Portugal. She describes her colorful work as "art on a budget", an ode to everyday objects and the way they interact while being put in the spotlight.

Yoann Siloine

Yoann Siloine is a French photographer who has been working in the fashion world for several years.

Andrew Seaman

Andrew Seaman is a photographer from Boys Town, Nebraska. You can follow him on Instagram (@amseaman) or see more of his photos at http://Andrews.photos

Heidi Yanulis

My name is Heidi Yanulis and I am a lifestyle and NGO photographer living in Antananarivo, Madagascar. I strive to help families, NGOs, and companies capture their unique experience of living and working on this incredible island.

Amarnath Tade

I'm a mechanical engineer student currently studying master of engineering in ECU, Australia. Photography is my favourite hobby since my childhood and always aimed to become professional photographer.

Zhan Zhang

Hi! My name's Zhan and I'm a photographer from the Bay area. I started as a self-taught photographer and it took a lot of time and effort for me to achieve my goals. Find what you love and keep working on it!

Zetong Li

Zetong Li grew up in China and came to California in 2012. Zetong currently works on building software products at a tech company in the Silicon Valley. His passion outside of work has been photography since high school.

More from Tolman Hall

Pair an award-winning novel with a Tolman Hall unit study for weeks of reading, writing, vocabulary, and cross-subject projects!

Find more Tolman Hall learning helps at Amazon, or visit us at www.TolmanHall.com.

Made in the USA
Coppell, TX
08 July 2022